MADE FOR MORE

A Journey of Discovery and Purpose

by

Bobby Benavides

Cover Art by: Katie Carowick

Edited by: Daniel Wilson

This book is dedicated to my family

My wonderful wife

Natasha and our awesome children,

Liam and Norah

With the hope that this will be a guide

to a better understanding of who you

are in the eyes of our Creator

And

The purpose you have for His glory

TABLE OF CONTENTS

ACKNOWLEDGEMENTS………….....…..........iv

FOREWORD by Chris Mullett……………….v

WHO AM I?...1

WHERE AM I?...25

WHAT AM I?...48

KNOWING THE GREAT I AM!....................63

CONTINUE THE JOURNEY……………….85

CONNECT WITH ME…………………….…87

ACKNOWLEDGEMENTS

The process of writing a book is strenuous. To accomplish the task I needed a supportive team around me. The first person I need to show   appreciation to is, my lovely wife Natasha. She has been so supportive and encouraging of my dream to write. She has pushed me to be better in life and writing. I am so grateful to have such a wonderful partner by my side.

I love you Natasha!

Secondly, I had to have a group of people   willing to look over my writing and give honest feedback throughout the process. There were   several who took time out of their busy lives to read over the several drafts and provide input and direction. I changed several paragraphs and rewrote the first chapter due to much of the insight I received from: Natasha B., Michelle D., Gabrielle J., Corryne D., Jonathan M., Karen A., Jane C., Jared SMB, Arnie A., Jennifer K., and Ray Nelly. Thank you for all your words of encouragement and wisdom.

Finally, for all who joined in the book launch team on social media. I am thankful for all of you! I hope it lives up to the months of posts with quotes and videos!

My family and friends have been so great and have inspired me to keep going. I cannot express my gratitude enough.

May you find as much joy reading this, as I have had writing it.

Peace and blessings friends!
Bobby Benavides

<u>FOREWORD</u>

Ten years ago Bobby Benavides and I met while working for World Vision Appalachia in Philippi, WV. Bobby had moved across the country from California (he's still a Raiders fan) and I had made a career change after 17 years of pastoral ministry and church planting. Both of us were in pursuit of God's calling and purpose for our lives. Both of us were at a place in our lives in which staying still was not an option. Both of us had decided that we were made for more. (See what I did there?) Bobby's geographical move and my professional move have put both of us in unique ministries. Bobby is blogging and writing devotionals and books, while I am the executive director of the Clarksburg   Mission, a homeless shelter in West Virginia.

So many people, especially Christians, wrestle with the question, "What should I do?" We tend to ask, "What is God's will for my life?" Throughout my years of ministry I've known a whole lot of people who are paralyzed by those questions. The more basic and important question is, "Who am I?" You see, once you answer the question about who you are, then you will know what to do. Made for More will guide you through the process of coming to terms with who you are in light of your relationship with the God who made you, pursues you, saves you and who now wants to use you to serve in the Kingdom of God.

Let's face it, most people live day to day answering to the loudest voice or the most urgent matter. We spend our days putting out fires. It is the rare person who is so sure of God's purpose and calling in their life that they seem to live life on a deeper level. Those people don't jump onto every spiritual wagon that comes along. They don't change direction so often that they never really get anywhere. The journey that you will go on as you read these pages, has the potential to make you one of those rare people who faithfully and steadily lives out God's purpose and calling.

I'm excited for you as you begin this journey. There is nothing more exhilarating than being in lock-step with God. I may be even more excited for the body of Christ that you have found this book. As each of us grow in our understanding of "who we are" and, therefore, we come to know "what to do," then we will be far more effective in being part of God's redemptive work in the world. We were Made for More and I'm thankful to Bobby Benavides for showing us how to get there.

Hope!

Chris Mullett, Master of Divinity, Candler School of Theology
Executive Director, Clarksburg Mission, Clarksburg, WV

WHO AM I?

WHO AM I?

I am almost positive you have asked yourself one of these questions, "Who am I?", or "Where am I supposed to be?", or "What in the world am I doing here?" These questions are heavy, but essential to discovering the path you are on, or should be on, while moving through the adventure called "life." For many of you, it has been a difficult path of discovery with nobody to talk things through. So, let us take a journey together, hopefully beginning the process of discovering the answers to these very difficult questions.

The first question is loaded, "Who Am I?" Many of you asked this question when you were in middle or high school. You looked at the friends you had and tried to figure out if you wanted to keep them or find others who might have been a better influence on you. You were trying to figure out your clothing style, your hairstyle, impressive words (that's so fetch!), whether or not you should have bought lunch or brought it, you know, the essential questions for life. The thing is, while contemplating the answers to those simple questions, you were answering the bigger question of "Who am I?" Essentially, every aspect of your middle and high school years helped form the answer to this question.

Now, as you have become older, you face deeper layers of this question. What defines you? What moves you? Who are you?! There is a deeper voice calling out saying, "I know who you are, and you are not it!" When you look in the mirror, do you feel like you are who you know you are supposed to be or capable of being? That is the question within the question of "Who am I?"

One of my favorite movies is *Zoolander,* starring Ben Stiller and Owen Wilson. Zoolander is comedic gold...at least to me. It is the story of a male model, Derek Zoolander (Stiller), who has been at the top of the male modeling industry for some time. He has made a profession of being "ridiculously good looking" and held the title of being top male model two years in a row, that is, until Hansel (Wilson) comes on the scene and becomes "so hot" and overtakes Zoolander for his title.

Losing the title of top male model sends Zoolander into an existential crisis. He runs out of the award ceremony in disbelief. He falls to his knees and views his reflection in a puddle and asks himself, "Who am I?" to which his reflection replies, "I don't know." He goes home in a state of depression and hides from the world.

Then, after an unfortunate event (his friend dying in a freak gasoline fight), Zoolander moves back home. He joins his dad and brothers in the coal mine and questions his existence again. After a commercial featuring Zoolander comes on in a bar, his dad becomes upset and degrades him for his modeling. Zoolander runs out of the bar, looks up at the sky, and asks the question, "Who am I"?

There is something intriguing about the different ways Zoolander approaches the question, "Who Am I?" The first time he asks the question, he asks himself and, of course, he had no idea. Then, the second time he asks, he looks up to the sky to seek the answer. After he looks up, his adventure begins.

Perhaps, this is where you are in your journey. You have this time in your life when you are trying to determine who you are and your purpose. Maybe you are ridiculously good looking, but you know there is much more to life than that…but what is it? You have something inside you telling you there is much more to life than what you are experiencing or living, and you know it is time for you to discover what that is.

You are on this journey of discovery. You are trying to figure out who you are made for and who you are supposed to be. Zoolander's experience is something you can relate to. You're at a point when you truly are trying to seek wisdom and direction. You have done it on your own for too long, and now, you need to look up and see what God has in store for you.

For many of you, you have made up your own design. You have thought about everything you believe you should have. You have great dreams; many will never become reality, but you dream. You even have made up scenarios in your head that would define your success. You have declared who you are, and when you don't match up to it, you will become defeated and disheartened. Many of you will become angry with God because the plans didn't work out, which is interesting, because you never included Him in the plans from the very beginning, but you're mad at Him.

When I was a kid, I remember imagining what I would be when I grew up. I remember wondering if I would have kids, marry the girl of my dreams, live in a mansion, and/or drive a nice car. All right, I played the elementary school game of MASH in my head...daily. I have a very active imagination, so I always had great times thinking about my future.

For those of you who don't know MASH, let me educate you on one of the best games either to depress fourth graders or raise their hopes they might be famous and on top of the world one day. Here are the basics: you draw a square on a piece of paper. On the top of the square, you write MASH (MASH was an acronym for Mansion, Apartment, Shed/Shack, or House). Then, on the right hand side, you write five names of girls you liked or, if you want to get extreme, your celebrity crushes. On the bottom, you write five numbers that would symbolize how many kids you would have. On the left hand side, you would write five cars you would like to drive.

Finally, you would have a friend close their eyes while you drew a spiral. When they said, "stop", you would count the lines you drew to find out your magic number. You would count with that number, starting at M, and move clockwise around the square as you eliminated items until you were left with one in each category. Inevitably, you would be in an apartment, with Meg Ryan, have seven kids, and drive a Corvette. Well, that was my game of MASH, at least, and it helped me realize, more than likely, my life would play out in a different way.

The fact is, the MASH game is how I would define myself at that age, and many of you define who you are by playing MASH in your lives now! You are not defined by the car you drive, the house or apartment you live in, the kids you have or don't have, or your marital status. Social media would have us believe our identity is found in those things, but that is not who we are!

So, who are you? Right now, I would ask you to take 20 seconds, go look in the mirror, and ask yourself that question; yes, ask yourself "Who am

I?" Did you do it? I hope you did, but this book is too riveting to put down, so most likely, you will wait until you're done. Some of you don't really know the real you. You need to introduce yourself to yourself. If you took the time to talk to yourself in the mirror, what did you hear? Did you experience anything? Did your tummy grumble? Did you have an epiphany? I would be impressed if you had one, but you could have. Let's face it; you really won't be able to discover who you are in twenty seconds, but you have started the journey.

Many of us don't take the time to listen or seek the answer to this question. You do what I just told you to do and expect something to be revealed in a short period of time. We can't even decide what we are having for breakfast in twenty seconds; how do you think you can figure out who you are in that time-frame?

Not all of us can be like Michael Jackson and find the answer "in the mirror", but it is a good start. So, where do we find the answer? God! God gave us a clear answer to this very important question, but not all of us have taken the time to read and embrace what He says about who we are in His eyes. It will definitely take longer than twenty seconds to read the Bible, but you can find amazing truth being spoken about who you are in a small amount of time if you just open the book.

For instance, in the second chapter of Ephesians, Paul shares:

"For we are his workmanship,

created in Christ Jesus for good works,

which God prepared beforehand,

that we should walk in them."

Ephesians 2:10 (ESV)

This points to the fact that humans are made by Him, in Him, prepared for something greater, to do good things in His name. Now that should be enough for all of us to say: "THAT'S WHO I AM!" Yet, unfortunately, many of you don't rest in that. You don't see yourself as made for a specific purpose. You cannot grasp that God has made you to be more than what you expect out of yourself. Why?

The answer to that question is found in scripture when Jesus shared, "The thief comes only to steal and kill and destroy; I have come that they may have life, and have it to the full" (John 10:10). Jesus says Satan, the enemy or "thief", will try to make us think we are limited. The enemy will try to make us feel inadequate to accomplish anything worthwhile in the kingdom of God. Satan will try to tell you who you are not and steal your ability to live a life worth something, but Christ is telling you exactly who you are and that your life is worth everything!

Christ has come so you can experience a full life, a life full of knowledge and grace, a life full of purpose and meaning, a life created by Him to reveal His glory. He came to earth to redeem creation and define who you are! Christ defined His people as "salt of the earth" (Matthew 5:13) and "the light of the world" (Matt. 5:14). We might look at salt as being unhealthy and causing high blood pressure, but Christ was comparing His followers to the original purpose of salt, which was to preserve and keep items fresh. He saw and sees you as a part of His preserving work on earth. He looks at you and sees someone with the ability to protect His world and assist in making the land healthy again. You are much more valuable in the eyes of your Creator than some of you believe, but you allow yourself to be defeated by the one trying to destroy your purpose.

The enemy is trying to put out the light by causing you to dwell on your past mistakes. He is trying to make you believe your "saltiness" is no longer worth anything because of your flaws. Christ is saying to you now, "Who you were does not define who you are to me!"

Another biblical example is found in the eighth chapter of John. One time, the religious leaders tried to trap Jesus by bringing a woman caught in the act of adultery to Him and sought His judgment against her. They expected Him to follow the law, which stated the woman should be stoned to death for such an act, but they were setting Him up, so they could bring charges against Him, according to His teachings. Jesus challenged them and said: "If any one of you is without sin, let him be the first to throw a stone at her" (John8:7). Nobody could throw the stone. No matter how strong the urge was to throw the first stone, they could not, and they walked away, leaving their rocks on the ground.

I can only picture it like this- the woman is still standing there with her head down, defeated, beat down, defining herself as an adulteress, and broken. However, Christ leans in and says, "Woman, where are they? Has no one condemned you?" She replied, "No one, sir," and Jesus tells her, "Then neither do I condemn you, go now and leave your life of sin" (John 8:10-11). He REDEFINED who she was! He made her into something new!

If Jesus was who He claimed to be, as the Son of God, then He had every right to be the one to condemn her. However, He did not put her down and He did not condemn her! He let her know who she was by saying, "Go now and leave your life of sin." That statement revealed her purpose BEYOND her past. This is how God works and moves in all of our lives.

Then, there is the account of Jesus with a Samaritan woman at Jacob's well, found in John chapter four. The interaction between Jesus and the woman created a new understanding of how racial divides are not a part of God's kingdom, how boundaries do not exist with God, and how your current life does not define who you are. Christ spoke candidly and honestly with the woman and, as he had with the woman caught in adultery, challenged her to discover who she was and His plan for her to live with purpose.

The narrative shares, Jesus arrives to the well, and He is tired. He sits down as the woman shows up in the middle of the day to retrieve water. The woman steps up to where He is sitting, and Jesus breaks the cultural barrier right away by making a simple request, "Give me a drink." Jewish people would not associate with Samaritans. They saw the Samaritans as dirty and untouchable. Jesus, as a Jewish rabbi, was definitely not supposed to speak to this woman, according to custom. However, her culture or race did not define her to Jesus, but what she offered Him defined who she was. He would soon reveal to her, even in her brokenness, she could provide thirst quenching water to a person in need.

He talked to her, describing the life-giving water He offered. He challenged her to think beyond her culture and social barriers to understand the value she had been given through the One who had spoken to her. Christ helped her see she was worth more than her personal life. He told her of the kingdom of God open to her, even if she was not a part of God's people (the Israelites) and had not been living a lifestyle that was honorable. He gave her new life by redefining what life means, not only to her, but to all of us.

For you fully and truly to answer the question of, "Who am I?" you need fully and truly to accept who God says you are. You are beautifully and wonderfully made for His glory. You are His workmanship, created to do great things for Him. He does not hold on to your mistakes the way you hold on to them. He will not look at you as being worthless and leave you as an outcast.

The religious leaders would have wanted to abandon and dispose of the woman caught in adultery. They would have loved to see her be defined by her mistakes, and if Christ had responded the way they wanted Him to, her life would have ended with her being remembered as an adulteress. The thief wanted to steal the joy from the woman at the well and make her believe her experience with Christ was not real and racial division still defined her. The enemy wants to ruin you and make you think you aren't capable of being used by God to do His work. The enemy wants to see you fail, but God wants you to succeed by finding hope in Him.

God showed all of humanity their value in the very beginning. God created the world. He made plants. He made the ocean and the sky. He made the animals of the earth. He gave life to everything. The entire time God created different pieces, He said it was "good", but when He made man, He stepped back, and looked closely and said "it was very good" (Gen. 1:31). He waited until that very moment to take His rest. His work was done, once He made His people in His image. He showed us our value from the start of it all! That is awesome!

When you allow others to say, "You won't amount to anything", when you give them power to speak negativity into your life, you hinder the ability of God's message of redemption and love to take root and guide you to who you truly are in Him. You are His. You are capable of so much more. You are made for so much more. Christ is looking at you saying, "You are my creation. There is nothing that can change that. You have been given life through me. You are worth everything I went through on the cross for you." It is up to you to accept that message.

So, when you look at yourself and ask, "Who am I?" may you know the answer is God's creation. You are God's masterpiece. You are the one He sees as very good. You are the one He knew from the very beginning and created to be used for His purpose. No one and nothing can change that definition unless you allow it. Trust His word and trust His message. You are made for Him. You are made for more. That's who you are!

WHERE AM I?

WHERE AM I?

So, now that you are thinking about who you are, let's talk about where you are. This is a huge question for many of you, especially those placed in roles that aren't fulfilling or facing a crossroads in life, regarding personal direction. Many of you have a feeling like you could do something more in your lives. You look to the future and cannot wait until you reach a certain milestone, be it graduating high school or retirement. You are marching forward with the end goal in mind. Yet, you might miss something great God is trying to reveal to you, right now, in the very place you don't want to be!

When I first entered youth ministry, I can remember hearing people say things like: "Just wait until you become a senior pastor!" or "How long do you plan on being in youth ministry?" or "Youth ministry is great, but will you start your own church someday?" What?! I mean, don't get me wrong; if God called me to start my own church or become a lead pastor of a church somewhere, I would do it, but if I focused on what could be, then I would miss the great things going on right in front of me as a youth pastor.

Before I took my first position as a youth pastor, I worked at a fast food restaurant. It was a fun time, and I made great friends. I knew I was meant to do something beyond that in youth ministry, but I did my job the best I could. I kept my sense of humor, had fun with my teammates, and never felt down about the fact I wasn't doing what I wanted to be doing. I knew God had a reason for placing me in that position for that time, and I needed to do it to the best of my ability.

To be honest, I took the job because the pay was great for an 18-year-old, and as a full-time employee, the benefits were solid. There was potential to move up and make more money. Yes, it was stressful, and I had hard days (some where my faith was not on display well), but I still aimed to work hard. I needed to pay for college, and the job was there. It was perfect for me at the time. I also had the chance to discuss faith with many of my teammates and show them Christians could be fun and enjoy life with people who may or may not believe what they believe. God opened many doors, and I learned much in that time that has carried over into my ministry experience.

The moral of my story is this: God's plan is way bigger than my plan or your plan. He will move you where He wants you to be when He wants to move you. Our responsibility is to do what He calls us to do, which is "…whether you eat or drink or whatever you do, do it all for the glory of God" (1 Cor. 10:31).

It's that simple. Where you are right now is exactly where you are supposed to be. Granted, some of you are in places because of your poor decision-making prior to following Christ, but God is still in control of that. He saw and knew the mistakes you made, but He also knew you would be where you are. He wants you to get to a point where you can accept His plan and move with His glory in mind. If you focus so much on what is to come, you miss what is happening in front of you right now.

Where are you right now? Look around. You might be sitting in your bed with your pillow behind your back reading this as you get ready to doze off. Maybe, you are in your office and you are growing weary, wondering when the promotion will come. Perhaps, you're sitting in a Starbucks, wondering whether you should take the job at Dunkin' Donuts. You are all in different places, and it is exactly where you are meant to be.

Let's take this a step further. Some of you look around at the craziness in the world and wonder when it will all end. You sit watching the news and hear of murders, terrorists, and hate-crimes and cry out to Jesus, asking Him to come back soon. You long for your future home because your current home is so broken. It is not wrong for you to long for your future home, but it is wrong to allow that longing to hinder you from doing things for the glory of God!

Many of you sit in a Church body listening to stories of missionaries and wish you could do what the missionaries do. You hear of people serving in war ravaged countries or locations lacking clean drinking water or places with people dying of curable diseases. Then, you leave thinking, "I wish I had the freedom to do what they're doing!" or "I wish I lived without fear like they do. I don't think I could do what they're doing!" Both thoughts are understandable, but incorrect!

Many Christians have bought into the misconception they have to go anywhere other than their current location to be a missionary. This has led to so many churches shutting their doors or being unproductive in their own communities. Jesus gave His disciples "The Great Commission", which is found in Matthew 28, and it says:

"All authority in heaven and on earth has been given to me.

Go therefore and make disciples of all nations, baptizing them in the name of the Father and of the Son and of the Holy Spirit,

teaching them to observe all that I have commanded you.

And behold, I am with you always, to the end of the age."-Matthew 28:18-20

Jesus calls His people to go into all the nations, but the disciples had to raise up leaders in communities to continue moving the message of Christ and growing their church THERE! Where you are now is your mission field! As the church serves their communities, new disciples are being made, which will lead to more people called to serve in different capacity for the glory of God.

Remember what Paul wrote in 1 Corinthians 10:31 "…whether you eat or drink or whatever you do, do it all for the glory of God." He wasn't talking about people eating or drinking in foreign countries. He wasn't saying, "Wait until you are in another location, then do it all for the glory of God." He was pointing the reader to the very reason they are where they are, to bring glory to the very One who places them where they are, right now!

So, what does this look like? How can you look at your current situation or vocation as a mission field? How can you be excited about where you are right now? These questions have easy answers, but they are not so easy for you to do. It takes action, personal reflection, and response.

Are you happy where you are? This is the first question you need to answer. If you are happy where you are, then you will be ready for the next step. If you are not happy with where you are, let's deal with that. Why? Is your boss a jerk? Do you have to do extra work for your co-workers? Are you underachieving? Do you think you deserve more? Here's my response. You may not like it, but the truth is…YOU NEED TO CHANGE YOUR ATTITUDE! You are expecting way too much out of broken people. Allow God to shape your heart into a heart that will see people as He sees them. He knows people are broken, but He is waiting for them to come to know Him, and He wants them to be where they are.

It is hard to look at where you are and rest in God's promises and trust He has you there for a purpose. My challenge to you is to remember He is present with you, where you are. At the end of "The Great Commission", Jesus told His disciples, "I am with you always." Earlier in His journey, He shared with His disciples there would be hard times if they chose to follow Him, and the same goes for all of us. He didn't come to make your life easier, but to make coping with life easier. This makes our eternity glorious.

This should help us see that where we are and how we view our situation can be used to shine light in the world for the glory of God. Being made for more is not about you. It is ultimately about your Creator. As you think about your current situation or vocation, do you view it as a way to draw people closer to God or do you allow it to hinder your ability to grow closer to God?

Let's get back to your attitude. When I say, "Change your attitude", I am not saying to change your attitude so you feel better or you can be happy. I am saying change your attitude because God expects you to. He has given you hope and a new life in Him, which means your current life is merely a time to reflect God to others. Your attitude should point people to Jesus. Your attitude should not be directly correlated to getting what you want, because you have already received everything you need. God will use your attitude about your current place to allow others to catch a glimpse of their Maker. Whether good or bad, your attitude points to Jesus. What reflection are you showing? What message is being sent to the people around you about the One you call Savior?

When you ask the question, "Where am I?" God wants to say, "Exactly where I put you." If you trust God is with you and is in control, then it should not be difficult to embrace where you are for His glory to be shown. When you accept this truth, you walk in joy, pointing to your Creator, no matter where you are. His purposes are great. His message is true. He places everyone exactly where He wants them.

You cannot allow yourself to ignore the significant question of, "Where am I?" God has made you for more, but this doesn't mean moving somewhere else. You can long to be somewhere else, but if you're trusting God, then you will wait for His plan to unfold for you. As for now, you are exactly in the place you need to be, celebrating Jesus and His purpose for you.

So, what happens when where you are isn't where you want to be? What happens when you look around and you find yourself stressed, frustrated, or irritated about being where you are? How do you handle it? What should you do?

Your current place might be a struggle or trial. You might wake up daily pushing yourself to get ready or even arriving to your place of employment. You might be searching for a job, trying to make ends meet, and getting frustrated because it seems like everyone around you is successful. This may cause you to question how you can be made for more, when you haven't been able to see much around you. This is a reasonable thought, so what do you need to do about it?

James 1:2-4 gives clear understanding of how followers of Christ should walk through trials and temptation. James begins by encouraging believers to "consider it pure joy when facing trials of many kinds." This is a hard concept to embrace.

Experiencing joy in trial is not how we are wired. We have become accustomed to allowing our trials to shut us down or even depress us. We turn to other things to help us through the trial. We lean on substances or relationships to help us cope with the tension of the trials.

People who cannot rest in joy become restless in life. They cannot find joy in their circumstances. They cannot find the work of God right in front of them. Yes, it might not be our ideal situation, but it is God's ideal way of revealing His purpose and plan for you and through you for others. Have you ever thought of that?

The message of James 1:2-3 is that of hope, strength, and perseverance in the faith through the stretching and tension discovered through trials.

Have you ever considered your life plan might not be God's life plan for you? His plan might be different, and He is waiting for you to embrace His plan and reveal His glory through it. The mess you might be living through could be the example another person needs to push through their trial. However, if you settle in bitterness or feeling sorry for yourself, then you miss the opportunity to share the joy of Jesus with someone searching for hope. You could be their last hope.

In James 1:9, the reader finds an encouraging word saying, "Believers in humble circumstances ought to take pride in their high position." The idea that God considers those in "humble circumstances" as people "in high positions" is against our logic. However, if you were rich or had everything you needed, you most likely would not even consider seeking God for wisdom or rest. Your joy would be found in your things and your success, not in the One who gave you the ability to succeed and ultimately defines your value. When you have money, fame, work, or anything else you have always wanted, you rest in your own abilities. You fail to see the work of God around you because you are looking at *your* work around you.

When you can find peace in your humble circumstance, then you can reach others in similar spots in life. Your story can enhance the story of another. Your failures and successes can allow others to see they too can make it. You need to be at a place in your life where you feel content and confident that God is in charge.

I have a little confession: I enjoy hip hop music. Actually, I really love rap music more than any other genre. I feel, some of the best poetry of life is revealed in hip hop lyrics, and I can gain great insight into the lives of those writing the lyrics and speaking them at one hundred miles per hour into the microphone. Another confession, I like Lil' Wayne. He doesn't always have the best lyrics, but he has great delivery, especially in his song, "Nightmares of the Bottom" on his album *Tha Carter IV*.

In the beginning of the song, he paints a picture of someone sitting at the top with everything they have worked for, and they are afraid to lose it all. Then he says: "We in the same picture, but we all got different poses." That preaches! You are all in

God's picture. It is bigger than you or anything you can imagine, but you all have different poses in His masterpiece. Your pose creates an amazing scene that God uses to reveal His message of grace and restoration.

It is time for another movie flashback. In the 1980's classic, *Back to the Future*, Marty McFly (Michael J. Fox) must go back in time to restore life as he knew it. There was a disruption in the present time when his mentor, Doc Brown (Christopher Lloyd), was murdered in a mall parking lot. He took the DeLorean time machine into the past to inform Doc of the impending doom. While visiting the past, he interacts with his parents and disrupts their potential relationship, which leads to a possible negative impact on the future of his family.

He had a photo of himself and his siblings, waving, that was affected by the relationship of his parents in the past. Every moment it seemed like his parents would not get together romantically, a body part would fade from the picture. As time went on, it seemed inevitable that Marty and his siblings would be erased from the future.

As the future changed, body parts faded. The picture was incomplete. The picture was the only way for Marty to see the influence he was having on his family. When you fail to see your value in the present photo, you might miss a grander tapestry being painted for you to enjoy.

Your present life matters significantly to God. If you clamor for the future and ignore the present, you might disrupt your path going forward. People need you to live your life fully now, where you are,

and who you are, for the fame of the One who put

you here.

WHAT AM I?

WHAT AM I?

René Descartes, often considered the father of modern philosophy, said these words:

"But what then am I? A thing which thinks. What is a thing which thinks? It is a thing which doubts, understands, affirms, denies, wills, refuses, which also imagines and feels.

(Meditation VI)[1]

Descartes also points out, "…I possess a distinct idea of body, inasmuch as it is only an extended and unthinking thing, it is certain that this I [that is to say, my soul by which I am what I am], is entirely and absolutely distinct from my body, and can exist without it." *(Meditation VI)* His thought process is interesting when you think about yourself as

---

[1] Excerpt taken from *Introducing Philosophy* by Robert C. Solomon

primarily spirit. Your soul is what makes you in this world. When you discover who you are in Christ Jesus, you come to discover what you are in this world and beyond. Your inner being is what lasts and is what God has rescued through His sacrifice.

Robert C. Solomon shares in his book, *Introducing Philosophy,* regarding Descartes' writing, "It is important to appreciate the kind of step Descartes has taken here. What he is saying is that self-identity depends on consciousness. Our identity does not depend in any way on our body remaining the same, and so human identity is different from the identity of anything else in the world."[2]

---

[2] *Introducing Philosophy (Solomon, Robert C., 2005, Oxford Press)*

These thoughts shared by Descartes and Solomon lead to your relationship with God. You are not meant to be on earth forever. Well, I guess if you look at scripture, you will see a new heaven and new earth, so you are meant to be here, but not in the form you are now. Your identity is not shaped by who you are, but what you are. Your identity is defined by how you view scripture from the lens of brokenness and ultimate healing.

This is a definitive point most of you will experience during your faith journey. You will realize God has declared you to be His child, which means you have been adopted into His family, and you now have a new way to live. We are a part of God's awesome story of redemption and grace. We are made new through Him.

Paul shared, "Therefore if anyone is in Christ, he is a new creature; the old things passed away; behold, new things have come" (2 Corinthians 5:17). In this verse, Paul is helping the church understand they are not what they used to be. They are defined by something new. Their bodies didn't change, but their spirit did. Their internal being that will last for eternity has been shifted by the power of love and hope in Christ Jesus.

This is what you are! If you claim faith in Christ, you are a new being, defined by the cross and resurrection. You are defined by His glory, not by what the world would define as glorious. You need not strive for things of this world because what you are is not of this world. Jesus said these words in Matthew 6:25, "For this reason I say to you, do not be worried about your life, as to what you will eat or what you will drink; nor for your body, as to what you will put on. Is not life more than food, and the body more than clothing?" What you put on your body cannot and will not make you whole. What you eat or what you own might have power to define you on earth because broken people have allowed that to occur.

However, you are not to worry about what defines you here, but ultimately, who will define you when you are gone. You are more than the clothes in your closet, money in your bank account, food on your table, your physical stature, or your looks. You have to accept the truth that what you are through Christ is worth much more than everything else on earth.

So, what are you? Yes, as Descartes said, you are a thinker driven by passion and desires. Perhaps, the real question isn't "What am I?" But maybe, "What drives me?" The discovery of your passion moves you. When you find out what you are excited about in life, then you discover your *what*.

I know people passionate about missions and service. They love going to a third world country or an urban community and loving people. They want to serve until their life is over, and even then, they will continue to serve while in heaven. This brings them great joy. They have discovered that service drives their answer to what they are. Their everyday job might not be in the capacity of being a servant, but when they get their chance, they take the opportunity to be involved in what they love.

Others are driven by teaching. They love to share the message of Jesus and teach people what it means and how to apply it to their lives. Again, they may not be in a vocational position to teach regularly, but excitement and energy flows through them when they discuss scripture.

We all have those things that drive us. You might be a fast food worker, but in your heart of hearts, deep within, you want to be serving teen moms. You would take any opportunity to walk alongside teen mothers who need to know love and acceptance from the body of Christ. You want to be that person. That's what you are.

You might be a CEO looking out the window of your top floor office, longing for the opportunity to be in a homeless shelter serving and loving people who have been neglected. Your heart yearns for when you can sit alongside people shunned or mistreated by society to help them experience new life in Jesus. That's what you are.

"What" you are, is what motivates you to continue going through life. Are you driven to do more because God has made you to be more? Are you moved to be more because Christ was the most for you? Your "what" is defined by your passions. God has instilled those thoughts in you that are meant to be shared and used. When you allow God to define your "what", then you will gain a new energy for doing what you love for the glory of God.

One thing Descartes said rings deep within me, "What is a thing which thinks? It is a thing which doubts, understands, affirms, denies, wills, refuses, which also *imagines and feels*."

The whole concept of being a thing that "imagines and feels" stirs deep within my soul. God has given all of us the ability to imagine possibilities. In the book of Acts, we find these words:

" 'And it shall be in the last days,' God says,

'That I will pour forth of My Spirit on all mankind;

And your sons and your daughters shall prophesy,

And your young men shall see visions,

And your old men shall dream dreams...'

(Acts 2:17) ESV

The fact that God is pouring out His Spirit on His creation to guide them in words of prophecy, dreams, and visions is amazing. He is moving all over the land causing people to think beyond their circumstances and discover what they are meant to do and be. They are discovering what the people of God can be. They are envisioning what a world would be like if the Church would rise up to what they could be to influence and enhance the world as salt and light.

The idea that you have the ability to feel is another example of God's way of allowing you to experience life through Him. You have a God who allows you to feel and see what He sees, if you walk with Him and abide in His ways. He has chosen to work in you to reveal empathy and compassion for the broken and lost. Your passions you are consumed by are rousing within because of the feelings God has given you so you may experience life in a whole new way.

There's a hard topic that must be discussed to grasp why you might not fully experience what I have been sharing with you. The only way to embrace what you are is through the work of Christ within you. The truth is, you are a sinful creature and the sinful side of you holds on to what Descartes recognized when he said, *"What is a thing which thinks? It is a thing which doubts, understands, affirms, denies, wills, refuses..."* In your sinfulness, you doubt God's ability to use you for what He wants. You deny the truth you are God's, and you willingly refuse to acknowledge what He has created you to be.

God is pushing through all of that with His Spirit. The Holy Spirit is moving inside you, trying to reveal what you are and what you can be in Christ. When you rest in your sinful self, then you deny your potential through Christ. You deny God's work in and around you for the good of creation and His glory.

God is beckoning you to discover His original purpose for you in this world. He is calling to those who will listen to allow them to see what they are meant to be in His kingdom. He is calling each and every one of you to discover what you are to Him-His vessels used to carry His message of hope, love, grace, mercy, redemption, and reconciliation to a lost world.

May you rise up to what you are and
acknowledge you are His, made for His glory.

KNOWING
THE
GREAT I AM!

KNOWING THE GREAT I AM!

So far, you have read about who you are, where you are, and what you are. Yet, I have not gone into enough detail about the One who has given you the answers to all these questions. In order to figure out what you are made for, you need to know the One who has made you. This should be the first priority for anyone who declares Christ as their Lord and Savior.

Let's take a glimpse at an Old Testament story found in the book of *Exodus*. The story of Moses has always intrigued me. Moses' story was fascinating from the very beginning. God had Moses begin his life in turmoil. The Pharaoh was killing male babies by drowning them in the Nile River to control the Hebrew population. When

Moses was born, his mother hid him for three months. When she couldn't hide him from the Egyptian soldiers, she put him in a basket and sent him down the Nile.

Then, Moses' sister followed the basket down the river to where the Pharaoh's daughter was bathing. The daughter picked up the baby, and as Moses' sister saw confusion on the face of the daughter, she told her she knew a Hebrew woman who could care for the child. It was Moses' mother! This is a crazy story right?! It gets better.

Now, I am sure it became obvious to those around the kingdom that Moses was not part of the Egyptian people, but he was accepted. Moses had to know he was Hebrew, not a true Egyptian, but you can infer that he came to grips with that reality. The

Pharaoh had the people of Israel enslaved in his kingdom. Since Moses was a Hebrew, he knew his people were being treated poorly, but he was in the kingdom and comfortable. However, at one point, he witnessed an Egyptian taskmaster beating a Hebrew slave and was driven to defend him. He killed the taskmaster, hid his body, and fled from the Pharaoh's kingdom after people found out what he did.

This is when it gets interesting, and really, this is where I want your minds to focus. After he ran away from Pharaoh, he stayed in Midian. While he was in Midian, the Pharaoh died, which opened a door for Moses to come back with possibly fewer repercussions waiting for him. However, something is said at the end of Exodus 2 that reveals God's heart for His people and who He is as a Creator:

"Now it came about in the course of those many days that the king of Egypt died.

And the sons of Israel sighed because of the bondage,

and they cried out; and their cry for help because of their bondage rose up to God.

So God heard their groaning; and God remembered His covenant with Abraham, Isaac, and Jacob. God saw the sons of Israel, and God took notice of them."

Exodus 2:23-25

God, in His infinite power and wisdom, heard their cries and groaning. He listened to His people. He remembered the covenant He made and "took notice." This is comforting to me and should be to you as well. You have a God who sees you and hears you in your pain and struggle. He is listening to you, and He knows your doubts and fears. He knows your concerns in life. He is listening and waiting for the right time to act, which might mean no action, but that is a whole other book.

In the midst of captivity, God was still present. He knew (and knows) what His people needed to get through the life they were living. He does the same for you. He sees something greater than you can when stuck in your time of struggle. While in slavery and doing hard labor, the Hebrew people were losing hope, while crying out for God to deliver them, but hearing nothing and not seeing anything beyond the dirt and heat they were working in. Contrary to that, God was working His plan and getting it in motion, seeing a bigger picture they could not see while struggling.

What does this say for you? How often do you miss significant things in life because you are so focused on your plight? You look at where you are and think there could be nothing more and there is no way God could love you or see you as anything worth saving. However, you see in the scripture above, you have a God who hears you and is putting a plan in motion to move onto the scene and deliver you from your suffering. God always sees more; we just have to be patient and rest in the truth of His omnipotence and omniscience.

Let's bring Moses back into the picture. If you have spent any time in VBS or Sunday school or with your grandma watching Charlton Heston holding up stone tablets, then you should be familiar with Moses and the burning bush. The interaction between God and Moses sets the tone for the rest of the story. God is in control, and He is choosing to use a man to do His work. These are the verses of the story I want you to focus on:

"The Lord said, 'I have surely seen the affliction of

My people who are in Egypt,

and have given heed to their cry because of their

taskmasters,

for I am aware of their sufferings.

So I have come down to deliver them from the

power of the Egyptians...

Therefore, come now, and I will send you to

Pharaoh,

so that you may bring My people, the sons of Israel,

out of Egypt."

Exodus 3:7-8,10

And

"But Moses said to God, 'Who am I, that I should

go to Pharaoh,

and that I should bring the sons of Israel out of

Egypt?'

Then Moses said to God, 'Behold, I am going to the

sons of Israel,

and I will say to them,

'The God of your fathers has sent me to you.'

Now they may say to me, 'What is His name?' What

shall I say to them?'

God said to Moses, 'I AM WHO I AM'; and

He said, 'Thus you shall say to the sons of Israel,

'I AM has sent me to you.'"

Exodus 3:11-14

Let's focus our attention on the first set of

verses. Again, God reiterates that He sees His

people in pain. He knows the need, and He is not

ignoring His people. When He says He has "given

heed to their cry", it's almost like He is trying to

soften Moses up for the task coming at him. His

heart had to be softened with empathy and

compassion. He had to understand the people in

slavery were God's people, and God would not

stand for them being in bondage any longer.

Moses would be the messenger for God to

reveal to His people He knew what was going on,

and He knew what He was doing. Now, it was time for Him to place Moses in his rightful position to recognize who God had made him to be and his purpose. Moses was made to be the leader of God's people. His purpose was to reveal the identity of the Hebrew people to put them in position to walk this world as God's chosen group.

I really enjoy the way God sets this up with Moses. He begins it in a similar fashion as when someone is asking you for a favor: "Alright, here is all the sad news and the amazing reason why I'm here", but then, He drops the bomb: *"Therefore, come now, and I will send you to Pharaoh, so that you may bring My people, the sons of Israel, out of Egypt."* Isn't that great! I mean, c'mon, that is a solid move by God. Moses is sitting, listening to how awesome God is and His great purpose in the world, but then the *BOOM*, "Hey! By the way, you're doing the work I need done!" I can only imagine his facial expression. There was probably a whole range of emojis flowing. Then, Moses responds, *"Who am I, that I should go to Pharaoh..."* This is how, I think, most of you reading would respond. That is, unless you're ultra-spiritual and have zero doubts. Then, honestly, why are you reading this?

All right, back to Moses' response. Isn't that accurate? I mean, think about it, "Hey God! Man, this is an awesome plan. I am super pumped. I can't wait to see how you free your people and stuff. Wait? What? Uhm...riiiggghhht! You're funny, God! Me?" This would most likely be my response.

I also find it interesting that he begins his response with the first question we addressed, "Who am I?" He needed God's clarification. He wanted to be justified by God to do such a task. He needed to hear God say, "I know what I am doing, and yes, you are the one I am choosing."

The self-doubt crept into his heart and mind. Moses could not wrap his thoughts around a God who could use a guy like him to do such a great work. I'm sure he was wondering how God could use him with his past. How could God use a murderer? What am I to these people but a guy adopted into royalty and didn't have to live like them? These questions are legitimate in the heart and mind of man, but God reveals a different perspective.

The next scene makes me laugh as we find Moses trying to understand what God is trying to do, and he decides to lay out a hypothetical scenario to God, "So, what if I go to them and then they ask me stuff about you? What then?" God probably smacked His forehead pretty hard, took a deep breath, and replied, "OH MAN! REALLY?! I didn't think about that?!" No, that's not what He said. He kept moving Him through the process, letting Moses know He will be there and He is "I AM."

Now, recognize something big happening here. Moses has only known Egyptian religious traditions. He might have heard about the Hebrew God, but had zero experience with Him. Now, he is face to fire with the One who created it all. He didn't know what to call God. He knew nothing about the covenant God made with Abraham, the father of the Hebrew people, to make him a great nation (Genesis 12), and the history of the people of Israel that came out of that covenant. He had to figure out whose voice he was hearing. So he asked the question, "Who are you?"

To take part in God's work, you should know the God you're working for. Moses was about to embark on a major journey and a trying experience, so before he took any steps, he wanted to be sure who exactly he was working for. Also, he knew trust would be an issue. So, he needed identification to give him authority to the Hebrew people. Therefore, God gives Moses the very name the Israelite people would know Him as going forward *YHWH* (Yahweh) or *LORD*, which would come from the Hebrew word that means "To Be." That is the only Hebrew lesson you'll receive the rest of your reading.

God had to place His authority over Moses for the work to go forward. He was, is, and always will *be!* This is how He will be known by His people and respected by the Pharaoh. He defined Himself to bring definition to the Hebrews.

You are like Moses. Moses was a man trying to find his place in life. He ran from his pain and tried to find comfort in unknown areas. He needed to discover his purpose and potential. He was lost. Before God made His move to speak to him, Moses was wandering with his sheep. Mankind wanders regularly. You are, most likely, in search of something bigger to be a part of. God is burning a bush in front of you, and He is ushering you in to participate in a great journey.

The great I AM knows you, but do you know Him? Do you know the One who has created you for great things? Do you know the One who defines who, where, and what you are? This is the question to ask yourself.

You might miss so much of what God has in store for you because you don't know His immeasurable love for you! Your eyes might be so focused on the pain of your past and your self-doubt that you are missing the burning bush telling you where to go. God has a plan, and He is working it out, but He is waiting for you to answer His call to step into the picture.

Let's fast forward to Jesus from Moses' story.
Again, just like the Hebrew people in captivity cried
out in Exodus, the whole earth was groaning and
crying out for a Savior. God heard the groans so,
just as He told Moses, *"I have come down to deliver
them from the power of the Egyptians"*, He came in
the flesh as Jesus. He declared to His entire
creation, while reading an ancient prophecy in the
temple:

"The Spirit of the Lord is upon Me,

Because He anointed Me to preach the gospel to the

poor.

He has sent Me to proclaim release to the captives,

And recovery of sight to the blind,

To set free those who are oppressed,

To proclaim the favorable year of the Lord."

Then He said…

"Today this Scripture has been fulfilled in your

hearing."

Luke 4:18-19, 21

Here, you will find Jesus declaring who He is for all the people to hear. His identity was made known. People were confused, but He knew who He was, is, and always will be for the people of God in the world He created. He then began choosing disciples, who had to know what He declared in the temple about Himself, and they followed.

It is all about knowing who you are following. God has given us identity and value, but if we don't know Him, then we can't follow His lead. Again, moving back to the story of the woman at the well found in the fourth chapter of John, the woman asked Jesus from whom or where she could receive living water. Jesus told her He was the source. Her life shifted when she discovered the Messiah, as will yours when you take the time to ask the questions so you may know Him more.

The deeper you grow with Jesus, the further you will go for Him. Essentially, you will go as far as you trust your leader.

As Moses sat at the burning bush, he gained trust in the words of God. The purpose of his time with God was to develop his faith to address the Pharaoh. He had to gain confidence in himself, through his Creator, to do the great work he was being called to do.

It is time for you to sit with God at the burning bush. Focus on His message to you. See your worth. Recognize the important role you play in this world for His glory. Rest in who He says you are. May you be willing to listen to the words of God in scripture, so you will be moved to experience who, where, and what you are, in Him. May you come to see you are made for more.

CONCLUSION

CONTINUE THE JOURNEY

The journey of life is long. You must be prepared to handle the ups and downs and everything in between as you traverse your way through it all. You need to think about all of these questions so you may have strength along the path.

The reality is, you can read all the books in the world, but the only way you can find the answers you seek is through the One who created you. Jesus is waiting for you to seek His wisdom. He longs for you to step into His story so He can influence yours. Your life will not be complete until you have come to grips with Whose you are and why you are made.

God has a great plan for you. He wants to reveal it. In fact, He already has started by having you open this book and reading to the end. Now, it's time to open His book (The Bible) and search out His message of truth, love, and hope. Truly listen for His Spirit's voice. Find a place of solitude and ask the questions you have.

Perhaps you will have your Zoolander moment? Listen closely after you ask the questions so your life adventure will truly begin. Enjoy the journey of discovery and purpose, for the glory of God.

CONNECT WITH ME

If you are interested in connecting with

me at any time, please subscribe to my

website @ www.bobbybenavides.me

Follow me on social media:

Twitter: @bobben74

Facebook: Bobby Benavides(@acalltoreconcile)

Instagram: @bobby_benavides

I would love to hear your thoughts on this

book and/or how I can be praying for you on

your journey!

Peace and blessings friends!

Bobby Benavides